Give Up!

Tina Albañez

Give Up!

by Tina Albañez

All rights reserved
ISBN 978-0-578-87992-5

For additional copies of this book contact:
Tina Albañez
tinaalbanez@icloud.com

All scriptures are taken from King James Version of the Bible unless otherwise noted.

Printed in the United States of America

"An interesting book with real-life applications on how to deal with such issues as frustration, worthlessness, and negativity…
The main idea is to "give up" or surrender your control to Him; and in so doing, you find the peace that only He can give.
Filled with instructional scripture and promises straight from the Word of God, you will be enlightened and encouraged at the same time!
I highly recommend this read!"
-Sis. Carol Porterfield

Special Thanks to...

My husband, Isai Albañez... Thank you for your constant love and support. You are my biggest fan and my voice of reason. I definitely would not have had the courage to see this come to pass without you!

Gage and JJ... You two give me more joy and strength than you will ever know! I am so thankful that I get to be your mom and watch the Lord doing mighty things in your lives!

Mom and Dad... To the ones who have always believed in me and supported me in every endeavor! You both are my rock! I am forever your baby girl!

Bishop and Sis. Porterfield... My journey with the Lord began with your guidance so many years ago. Thank you for your continuous love and encouragement!

Pastor Cory and Sis. Amelia Porterfield... I am so blessed to call you my pastor. Thank you both for being wonderful examples of God's loving hand in action.

Mandy, Brandon, & Stephanie... To the best siblings ever! I am so thankful to know that you will always be in my corner!

Andrea, Beth, Melinda, Melissa, Paula... To my best friends for more than thirty years! Our friendship means so much to me. You are my constant support system!

Introduction

From a very young age, we learn phrases like "Never Give UP"! "Don't be a quitter"! Although I do believe that this is a good concept when it comes to working toward achieving life goals and believing the Lord for the answers to our prayers, I have come to understand that we shouldn't always live with this mindset.

What if I told you that there is a time when it's ok to **Give Up**? What if Giving Up is the best decision you could make?

Life is not fair and sometimes we find ourselves struggling through storms that we cannot navigate. These storms can also leave us damaged; washed up onto life's shore without a clear direction of how to move forward. Those are the times that we must decide to **Give Up** to the Lord all the damaging emotions that we can't control. In doing so, we can allow the Lord to replace them with His love, peace, and acceptance.

Through this book I will share with you some personal testimonies of how I have had to learn to **Give Up** to the Lord plenty of emotional baggage that life has left me with. I will also share with you scriptures of promise that have helped me navigate through the storms. I pray that you will find it relatable and helpful in your own personal journey with the Lord.

Content

Special Thanks-........................... 5

Introduction…................................ 7

Chapter 1- The Struggle………… 11

Chapter 2- Give Up Confusion…. 25

Chapter 3- Give Up Worthlessness……………………… 35

Chapter 4- Give Up Jealousy…… 51

Chapter 5- Give Up Frustration…. 63

Chapter 6- Give Up the Past……. 77

Chapter 7- Give Up Negativity… 89

Chapter 8- Give Up Bitterness… 99

Chapter 9- Give Up Excuses….. 113

Chapter 10- Conclusion……. 123

Chapter 1

The Struggle

The Struggle

She found herself in front of a beautiful ocean one day. As she stood there at the edge of the beach, feeling the water occasionally splash her feet, she remembered why this was one of her favorite places to be. It was so peaceful and majestic. As she walked out into the water, she breathed in the fresh air and the waves felt good up to her knees. She had always considered herself a good swimmer, so she decided to take advantage of this opportunity and immerse herself into the water for a swim. When she came up, she was a little confused at what she saw. How could that quick swim have taken her so far away from the security of the beach? Suddenly land seemed so far away and she found herself beginning to panic! She tried to begin swimming back to shore, but all of a sudden a huge wave pushed her out farther. It seemed like the harder she tried to stay above water, the more the current was pulling her under. Then it happened... Another large wave came and pulled her all the way underwater! She struggled with which direction was up to get that desperately needed gulp of fresh air! Then she heard a voice say "Give Up". Give up? Never!

That wasn't in her nature. You see she had been through a lot of things in her life. She had also failed at a lot of things. But she had never given up! She was not a quitter!

There is no doubt that the enemy has whispered those words in your ear on more than one occasion, just as he has mine. "Give Up". But the question I'm asking you and myself today is... <u>Whose voice is it?</u>

The truth is, life on this earth is hard and that will never change. Maybe some of us thought that when we became a Christian that life would get easier. But in reality it didn't because as long as we live in a sin filled world, this side of heaven, we will always face problems, storms, test, and trials. The wonderful news is, as Christians, we don't have to go through them alone and fight the battles this world throws at us with our own strength. We have our Lord and Savior Jesus Christ to fight for us! The One who never loses! The One who is always Victorious!

But thanks be to God, which giveth us the Victory through our Lord Jesus Christ.
(1 Corinthians 15:57)

For whatsoever is born of God overcometh the world and this is the victory that overcometh the world, even our faith. (1 John 5:4)

I don't know about you, but the problem that I sometimes have is that in the middle of the storm or battle that I'm in, I can't always see the Lord working. I have figured out something about myself over the years. **I am a fixer.** I'm sure many of you are too, especially if you are a mom. Some people, whether they are a parent or not, are peace makers, or problem solvers by nature. I'm sure many of you can relate. We always have to fix problems and situations that come up in everyday life. It's just what we do. I mean, think about it, when our children have a problem, who do they come to? Us! And nothing in this world makes us happier than when we are able to fix a problem that our kids have! When we put that band aid on a cut on their arm, or help them with their homework project at school. And I guess being a first grade teacher, makes this so true for me. I have a room full of six year olds that I spend my days with, solving problems and situations that come up all day long.

So what happens when we know God CAN fix our problem? We know what the Bible says! We know we serve The One who has All Power in HEAVEN and EARTH! We even have that FAITH that the scriptures talk about that He will fight our battles for us, BUT we just don't see it happening! And there is that voice in our head again "GIVE UP". What?

I have come to understand something recently that has helped me tremendously when I find myself in this situation. **There is a difference between <u>faith</u> and <u>trust</u>.** In my mind and my walk with God, I had always used these words as if they meant basically the same things. I'm sure I have even substituted one word for the other. What I have learned is that <u>faith</u> is believing that God **can** and even **will** answer my prayer, but <u>trust</u> is actually handing my problem over to Him and trusting Him completely to do it.
WITHOUT MY HELP! OUCH!

Oh yes, this is the tricky part right? I mean, if we are honest with ourselves, we can have that "mountain moving" faith because we know how powerful our God is and that He is ABLE to fix any situation!

But do we truly trust Him enough to take our hands off of it and allow the Lord to complete the process and answer our prayer in His own way and timing?

The only way that I have been able to do this is by reading, studying, and knowing what the Bible says about this!

For my thoughts are not your thoughts, neither are your ways my ways, saith the Lord. For as the heavens are higher than the earth, so are my ways higher than your ways, and my thoughts than your thoughts.
(Isaiah 55:8-9)

I want to pick up now with the story that I began with. Maybe you are wondering what happened to this girl. Did she listen to that voice telling her to "Give Up" while she was struggling for her life? The answer is YES! She did listen to the voice! She did **Give Up**! And it was the best decision she ever made aside from giving Christ her life all those years ago!

Please let me explain.

I have never been the person who has visions from the Lord. I try my best to walk closely with the Lord daily through prayer, fasting, and the studying the Word of God, as I'm sure many of you do. Maybe some of you have had visions, but I never had. That's why at first I wasn't sure of what this was that the Lord was showing me and why. My most recent battle that I have been in has rocked me to my core. So recently I just began seeing this story about the girl at the ocean play out in my mind, then I realized that *IT IS ME*! I do love the ocean. Although we are not really beach people, as far as spending week long vacations there, we do try to visit this one place in Mexico every time we go visit family. It is my favorite place to go on our trips and I always look forward to seeing the ocean and God's beautiful creation! I began to realize that this is the perfect analogy of my life that God is showing me. It all happened so fast. One minute I was enjoying this beautiful life that God has given me living for Him and serving Him alongside my wonderful husband and two boys.

Then when I came up for a breath of air, I couldn't believe what was happening. The waves of life had swept me out so far that I couldn't get back to the security of land.

I won't go into details of this storm in my life because it is still not over. But to help you understand the intensity of it, I will tell you that it involves my children. If you are a parent, (especially a mother) now you can relate. When this storm began my boys were the ages of 14 and 19. I was watching hell being unleashed on them. My husband and I have raised them in church and living the life of ministry their entire lives. But the pressures that are put on pastor's kids are very real. And the traps that the enemy sets for them are as well. So being the mom, the fixer, the helper that I am, I wanted and tried so desperately to help them. I prayed, fasted, and believed that God could deliver them out of these situations! I began to question myself when I didn't see the results that I expected.

Why was I still so far out in this ocean, struggling for my life it seemed? Gasping for air! Fighting, so desperately, for my own (spiritual) life! And to make it worse, I kept hearing this voice telling me to "Give Up"! Me? Never!
Give up my kids? Not this Mama!

When you're in the middle of a struggle that is so intense many times it's hard to tell where the voices are coming from.

When I really took the time to listen closely I realized it was not the voice of the enemy trying to kill me. It was the voice of my Heavenly Father telling me to "GIVE UP"! In this "vision" that the Lord was showing me, I could see this scene playing out from a distance. I could see the Mighty Hand of God right directly under me while I was thrashing about in the water struggling to hold on! Then I realized He was showing me that He is there, WAS there, the whole time ready to catch me and take control of this awful situation that I was living through. But as long as I kept splashing about trying to keep my hands on it and refusing to **Give Up** my control, I was not allowing the Lord give me the peace and security of His Hand!

So yes Lord, I "GIVE UP"!
I Give Up…
My control
My confusion
My frustration
My pain
My heart ache
My fear

It's then that I learned the difference between FAITH and TRUST!

I had the faith to believe God was able to answer my prayers, but I did not fully trust Him enough to **Give Up** and allow Him to do it.

As moms, it's hard to understand that there actually is someone who loves our children more than we do. But God does! HE formed them and knew them before we did! The Lord reminded me also that as tiny babies, I dedicated both my children back into His loving arms! So yes Lord, I **Give Up**! They were yours first!

Now does this mean that from that day that I let the Lord save me from my horrible situation that everything is perfect now? Absolutely not. But I do trust my Father with the children He gave me and I am learning to trust the process.

Proverbs 3:5 has always been one of my favorite scriptures. I memorized it many years ago and it has kept me through plenty of storms. But it has taken on even more meaning in my life personally since I have been learning to truly "Trust in the Lord".

Trust in the Lord with all thine heart, and lean not unto thine own understanding.
(Proverbs 3:5)

Through the next few chapters my prayer and desire is that I can help you understand that there is so much freedom and peace that comes along with **Giving Up!** Along the way I will share some testimonies of how the Lord has used some horrible situations to break me and rebuild me into who He wants me to be. I am definitely still a work in progress, but I have learned to **Give Up** many things to the Lord over the years. And each and every time God has been faithful!

Chapter 2

Give Up

Confusion

Give Up Confusion

Throughout my life I have been faced with some very difficult and confusing situations, as I'm sure many of you have. One of the lowest times in my life was when I had to face the nightmare of the murder of one of my best friends at the age of 20. I know we hear stories about these things happening, but we never think it's going to happen to anyone close to us. It was one of the darkest times in my life. I had so many questions for God. Why? "Why Lord, would you allow this to happen to her? She was one of the sweetest souls that you ever created." But the Lord, so carefully and lovingly carried me through that time. I learned that as long as we live in a sinful world, awful things will happen to wonderful people. It is during those times of brokenness, when we can't find the strength to look up some days, that God works best inside of us! If we will give Him our broken hearts, we will learn that He is the Master builder. He is the one who can take the shattered pieces of our heart and life and use it to rebuild us. He will make us stronger, more compassionate, loving, and giving. But most of all He will pull us closer to Him!

Oh, how we long to be closer to the Lord don't we?

I mean we pray that. We desire that "closer walk" with God. But the sad truth is we don't want to have to experience the brokenness that it takes to get us there!

But now, Oh Lord, thou art our father, we are the clay, and thou the potter, and we all are the work of thy hand.   (Isaiah 64:8)

I remember being so confused with my life during the time of Kristy's death. I was confused about my purpose in life. I was confused about my walk with the Lord and my eternity. And when this tragedy struck I was so confused about why God let this happen. My heart ached for her parents, family, friends, and really an entire community as we grieved this horrific loss. I can honestly say that it was during this time of confusion and brokenness in my life that I allowed the Lord to come in and truly be my Lord and Savior! I'm so grateful that I didn't stay stuck in that confusion, but I allowed the Lord to use it to draw me closer to Him. I allowed Him to be The Potter and I was that broken piece of clay in His hands.

My heart still aches for her parents, but my prayer is that they could find some kind of comfort in knowing that Kristy not only touched so many people in her life, but she also changed my life by her death.

At the age of 20 I was in a place in my life where I was seeking something from the Lord. I really didn't even know what I needed from Him. I just knew somehow that I wasn't satisfied. I had gone to church with my parents as a child and new about God. I learned all the Bible stories in Sunday School. This made me curious and made me want to know more about God. I felt a tug at my heart at a very young age. I did what I was told that I needed to do and asked the Lord into my heart as a child. I immediately felt better. I felt closer to the Lord. As I got older and into my teenage years, I began feeling like something was missing in my walk with God, but I didn't have a clue what to do about it. After high school, I can remember beginning to feel very anxious about my eternity. I really didn't know why I was feeling this way because, after all, I had done everything that I had been told was my path to salvation and living in the Peace of God.

I had confessed my sins, asked the Lord's forgiveness, and asked the Lord to come in and live in my heart.

Let me stop here for a moment and say that the purpose of writing about my experience with salvation is in no way intended to confuse or diminish anyone else's own experience. This chapter is about **Giving Up Confusion**. I am giving you my personal testimony of how the Lord used a horrific tragedy to draw me closer to Him!

Confusion! It is a dangerous emotion that many times is overlooked in our lives. We like to look past it and make excuses for its presence. Like many things, we just tolerate it for a while, until we get used to it. Then, before we know it, we are welcoming it into our home. We tell ourselves things like "I'm just so busy." "I just have too many things on my mind." "One day, life will slow down and I will feel better." But let me warn you that confusion does not come from God. It is, however, one of Satan's most used weapons!

For God is not the author of confusion, but of peace, as in all churches of the saints.
(1 Corinthians 14:33)

I can remember during the time after Kristy's death, actually crying myself to sleep at night because I had let this confusion turn into a real fear about my eternity. I would pray and ask the Lord to lead me to the answers that my soul so desperately needed. I longed for that "Peace of God that passes all understanding". I knew that there had to be more to this walk with God, but I had no idea where to look! Then one day someone invited me to church with them. It was a church that I knew nothing about. I did, however, know the person who had invited me before and after they began going to church there. I had seen a complete change in their life for the good. They carried that Peace that I was seeking with them. And I knew that was what I needed. So the following Sunday I went with this friend to Jesus Name Community Church. When we got there the service had already started.

As I walked into the building and heard the praises of the Lord being lifted up in song by the congregation, I had a feeling that I can't explain come over me that I was finally home. This kind of worship and praise to the Lord was foreign to me, but at the same time it was exactly what my soul had been looking for! Not long after that, I completely surrendered my life to the Lord and received the beautiful gift of the Holy Ghost with evidence of speaking in other tongues, and was baptized in the Name of Jesus Christ! If you have had this experience, then I don't need to tell you how impactful it is to your life! If you have not, and you are open to the possibility that the Lord could have more for you, then I would urge you to seek out the answers you are looking for. Don't settle or tolerate any confusion when it comes to your walk with God. I am so thankful that I was able to **Give Up** the confusion in my life!

Then Peter said unto them, Repent, and be baptized every one of you in the name of Jesus Christ for the remissions of sins, and ye shall receive the gift of the Holy Ghost. (Acts 2:38)

If you are dealing with confusion of any kind in your life right now, I want to encourage you to resist it by praying and seeking the Lord with all of your heart. And allow the Lord to take that brokenness you have experienced and use it to make you into someone new!

And ye shall seek me, and find me, when ye shall seek me with all of your heart.
> *(Jeremiah 29:13)*

Ask, and it shall be given you, seek, and ye shall find, knock, and it shall be opened unto you.
> *(Matthew 7:7)*

Chapter 3

Give Up Worthlessness

Give Up Worthlessness

Sometimes in life, we are faced with the having to pick up the pieces of our life that someone else has shattered and left us with. I found myself there. The place I never dreamed I would be. I always, naively, thought that if I loved enough, forgave enough, and fought enough for my marriage that the end result would ultimately be in my hands. But there I was, face down on the floor of life, trying to pick up all those tiny fragments of myself that I was left with. Then I was faced with the daunting task of putting them back together in some way that resembled the old me. But God had other plans! It didn't take me long to realize that those pieces were so tiny, so broken, that I would never be able to do it. I am so thankful that we serve the Master Potter, the Master Builder! I'm so thankful that my God specializes in taking broken things and making them new!

Therefore if any man be in Christ, he is a new creature: old things are passed away; behold, all things are become new.
(2 Corinthians 5:17)

If you have been faced with, or been through, "the D word", then you can relate perfectly to what you just read. Yes, I'm talking about that dreadful word that so many people cringe over when they hear (especially in the Christian world)....

DIVORCE.

I believe with all my heart in the sanctity of marriage. I also know that the majority of people who find themselves in a failing marriage never expected it to end the way it did as they stood before their future spouse on their wedding day and vowed their love to them.

There is really no way to be able to truly understand the fear, confusion, and guilt that someone goes through when living through a divorce if you have never experienced it. If you haven't, you may have watched someone you love suffer through it. There are so many damaging emotions that they are forced to sort through, when it is all said and done.

In my situation the enemy used all of those bad emotions against me. And it's sad to admit that I played right into his trap. The truth is there's no such thing as an easy divorce. Yes, some are uglier than others, but even though I knew that, biblically, I was not bound to them anymore, because of infidelity, I still carried around so much guilt and shame.

I'm going to be completely honest right now. It has been 20 years since I went through this and even as I am typing this all these years later, that knot in my stomach is back. The enemy is whispering in my ear to skip this chapter and not talk about it because people are going to read this and judge me. But I will keep going because this book is not about protecting my feelings. It's about trying to help someone who might be struggling with breaking free of some of these chains of emotions that can bind us and keep us from really living the life that God has planned for us.

Let me share some things with you that helped me to **Give Up** my fear of judgement, my heartache, and my pain. I pray that this will help you as well.

Maybe your struggle doesn't come from the same place as mine. Maybe your feelings of guilt, pain, and worthlessness come from an abusive childhood. Maybe you've lived through a life of addiction, or a number of other horrible things that life can throw at you.

First of all...

*Get yourself a support group.

I'm not talking about a group of strangers that you confess to once a week. I'm talking about surrounding yourself with people who you know have your back. Find people who love and believe in you. I am so blessed to have amazing parents and family that helped me. I also had the love and support of my pastor and pastor's wife, church family, and close friends. I cannot stress enough the importance of having positive people surrounding you when you are struggling with these hard emotions.

The enemy would love to remind you of how cruel people can be, but the truth is that there are good people in this life that will love and support you!

Second...

Get involved in your church/community.
The worst thing you can do is be alone when you are fighting feelings of fear, guilt, and pain. I found that giving of my time and energy to others was very helpful. When you look for good causes to invest your time and energy into, I have no doubt that you will find plenty to choose from.

Third...

Pray and study the Word of God.

The more time you are spending with God, the less the enemy will be able to confuse you about your worth. Find scriptures that are encouraging and pray them over your life. There is something so powerful about praying the Word of God!

For I know the thoughts that I think toward you, saith the Lord, thoughts of peace, and not of evil, to give you an expected end.   (Jeremiah 29:11)

Giving up Worthlessness

I realize this chapter is titled "Give Up Worthlessness", and I haven't spoken much about that specific emotion yet.

I am going to be very vulnerable with you right now. I'm about to share with you something that I went through that I am not proud of. I was having thoughts that I am embarrassed to say that I actually entertained for a short time. This is not easy for me to share because even some of the closest people in my life don't know about it. But if I can help someone overcome these feelings of abandonment and worthlessness, that I know all too well, then it will be worth my discomfort in writing about it.

For something to have worth means that it is useful for something. I will tell you that there was a period of time in my life that I truly believed that I was useless and it would never change. The enemy came in during my most vulnerable time and pounced like that "roaring lion" the Bible refers him to.

Be sober, be vigilant; because your adversary the devil, as a roaring lion, walketh about, seeking whom he may devour.
(1 Peter 5:8)

*I'm positive that someone reading this has felt this way before.

The enemy doesn't play fair! His favorite thing to do is kick us when we are down. He does that by flooding our mind with lies about our worth and our (lack of a) future.

As I told you earlier, I began truly living for God at the age of 20. I had felt a calling on my life for mission work almost from the beginning. I had read books about missions and missionaries. I was able, with the help of my church family and friends, to go on a mission trip to Australia at the age of 22. I came back from that trip a different person. My draw to this kind of work was more intense.

I can vividly remember lying on the floor one day during one of my many pity parties after my divorce. (Believe me, these are things I am not proud of but I'm trying to be completely honest in hopes of relating to someone.) I remember all of those feelings of worthlessness and fear of never being able to be used by the Lord flooding over me! It was during that time that Satan began to go even further. He began to put thoughts in my mind that not only was I worthless, but since my life had no meaning or purpose now, "Why keep living it?" Like I said the enemy will fight dirty! I am ashamed to say that I actually did entertain that thought for a moment.

But I am so thankful that the voice of the Lord was louder in my life at that time than Satan's voice! I remember crying out to the Lord that day and asking Him to help me fight these worthless feelings. I told the Lord that I didn't know what my future looked like, but I knew that just being His child was enough reason to live!

Maybe you are reading this and can relate based on your own personal circumstances. Maybe the enemy has kicked you while you were down.

Maybe, like me, you were so ashamed that you actually believed those lies even for a brief moment! If so, let me encourage you today! You are enough for the Lord! You have so much WORTH in His eyes! You are the "apple of His eye"! I am so thankful that we serve a God who loves us unconditionally and loves taking broken messes and making them into something beautiful for His kingdom!

... for he that toucheth you toucheth the apple of his eye.
(Zechariah 2:8)

Keep me as the apple of the eye, hide me under the shadow of thy wings.
(Psalm 17:8)

I can't end this chapter without telling you how God's plan for my life played out. Fast forward a few years... Lord brought a man to our church from Tecate, Mexico. His name was Isai Albañez. Our church had just begun a Spanish ministry and he was called here to help lead it.

I think we were interested in getting to know each other after some time, but there was one big obstacle. We couldn't talk to each other! Ha-ha! Yes, I'm convinced the Lord has a sense of humor! Isai only spoke Spanish and I only spoke English.

Long story, short... With the help of some great friends and some awkward "dates" where someone had to translate for us, we ended up learning how to speak to one another, falling in love, and have been married for 17 years now! I can remember so vividly asking the Lord to send me someone who loved God more than me. Because I knew that if he did then he would love me the way I needed to be loved. Wow! God is so good and faithful! I can honestly say my husband loves the Lord first and me and our children next more than anything! Oh, and that calling to mission work that I knew I had all those years before? God has a way of completing His plan for us that we could never imagine! I have been serving alongside my husband who is the pastor of Centro de Adoración Familiar for 17 years now.

This is the church that blossomed from that small Spanish ministry all those years ago. Over these years working and serving in this ministry, I have realized that this is my mission field. The Lord brought it here to me.

I love my church family with all of my heart and love being a part of what God is doing in the Hispanic community!

Let me encourage you today that you have so much worth! This book is about Giving Up, to the Lord, those things that are holding us back from living the life that God has planned for us. So let's **Give Up** that pain, fear, doubt, and yes, WORTHLESSNESS! And in return the Lord will give us His love, peace, and purpose in life!

And we know that all things work together for the good to them that love God, to them who are the called according to His purpose.
(Romans 8:28)

Chapter 4

Give Up Jealousy

Give Up Jealousy

I know when we hear the word jealousy, we usually think of a romantic relationship. It could be as simple as a high school crush who you saw talking to another girl, or as complicated as infidelity in a marriage. I think we can all agree that, no matter which side of the pendulum we fall on, jealousy is one of the most damaging emotions that we can entertain in our lifetime. It will absolutely consume our every thought! If we are honest with ourselves, I'm sure we can all admit that we have struggled with this emotion at some point in our lifetime. We can also agree that it can put such a strong hold on us that we actually turn into someone that we don't recognize. I know I have had my own battle in the past with jealousy. I have come to realize that one of the reasons that we sometimes entertain this emotion so easily is because we feel justified in doing so. After all, "it was THEIR fault!"

"He should not have talked to her." "I saw him giving her *that* look!" And my *go to*... *"Well, I know what he was thinking!"*

The type of jealousy that I want to address with you today, though, is not romantic jealousy. It is a type of jealousy that I feel is much more common and easily disguised in our society today. For this reason it can easily spread, like a virus, infecting one Christian after another. I am convinced that his type of jealousy, just like romantic jealousy, stems from a lack of self-confidence or self-worth. **It happens when we compare ourselves to others.**

I can write about this today because it is something that I have fallen into in the past. And if I don't pay close attention to it, I can easily let it creep back into my daily life. The sad truth is that our society is set up for us to automatically compare ourselves with others. Everywhere we look we see ads and commercials trying to get us to purchase something in order to live up to someone else's status. It is very subtle.

If I don't really pay attention to my emotions I can see that pretty dress that my friend is wearing and instead of feeling happy for her, I find myself jealous that I don't have one that nice. The Bible addresses this as a SIN. It is called COVETING. The Lord knew that it was going to be such a problem in our lives that He made it one of the Ten Commandments!

Thou shalt not covet thy neighbor's house, thou shalt not covet thy neighbor's wife, nor his manservant, nor his maidservants, nor his ox, nor his ass, nor anything that is thy neighbor's.
(Exodus 20:17)

One thing that I notice about this commandment is that the Lord specifically lists things that He knew people would be jealous over. He didn't just say "Thou shalt not covet". He got specific. And at the end of the verse He decides to cover it all! *"... nor anything that is thy neighbor's."* I believe this is important to recognize. Let me repeat… this sin was so important to the Lord that He made it a commandment!

I believe we have to make a conscious effort to avoid falling into this. Or at least I know I do. I will tell you something that I started doing that has helped me keep a handle on this emotion. Whenever I see something that someone has and start to feel that envy, jealousy, or begin to wish I had something that is theirs, I will actually begin to make myself pray for them and thank God for blessing them! I immediately feel better and notice those bad feelings are instantly gone! I can just imagine how furious it makes the devil when I do this! You see, the Lord does not want us competing with one another. He wants more than anything for us to love and care for one another!

A new commandment I give unto you, That ye love one another, as I have loved you, that ye also love one another. By this shall all men know that ye are my disciples, if ye have love one to another.
(John 13:34-35)

This is my commandment, that ye love one another, as I have loved you.

(John 15:12)

Be devoted to one another in love. Honor one another above yourselves.

(Romans 12:10 NIV)

We were not created to have these feelings of jealously. We were, however, created to be thankful for the things we do have!

In every thing give thanks: for this the will of God in Christ Jesus concerning you.

(1 Thessalonians 5:18)

The truth is, I really do love people and want the best for them by nature. And whenever the devil tries to plant that seed of jealousy or envy in my mind I refuse to cultivate it! Let's decide to pluck it up and destroy it with our prayers and encouragement for one another!

Life is not a competition! Let's be thankful to the Lord, always, for what He has blessed us with and cheer on everyone else as the Lord blesses them!

I can't help but believe that it makes the Lord smile and be proud of us as His children when we support one another. Think about how you feel when your children don't get along. As a parent, it makes my heart hurt to see them fighting or arguing, or even just not supporting one another. I know it has to break God's heart when He sees us doing the same thing to one another.

*Life is not a competition! Yes, it is a race, but we are all on the same team! We are all working toward the same goal.

So let's help and encourage one another along the way!

I know what some of you may be thinking because the thought has crossed my mind a time or two if I am honest. **Some people make it really hard to cheer them on.** We all know who they are. I'm sure one or more people have already popped into your mind when you read that sentence. Those people who seem to have too much self-confidence. They are boisterous and proud. They love to brag about all of their accomplishments and make you feel less than them.

I am so glad that the Bible has an answer for every situation that we face (even if it's hard to swallow sometimes). The Lord tells us to love and pray for them as well!

But I say unto you, Love your enemies, bless them that curse you, do good to them that hate you, and pray for them which despitefully use you, and persecute you... For if ye love them which love you, what reward have ye? Do not even the publicans the same?
(Matthew 5:44&46)

If we really want to be like Jesus then we can't only love those who love us first. Jesus loved everyone unconditionally and expects us to do the same. Is it easy? Definitely not! But the Lord did not tell us that this Christian life would be easy. On the contrary, He warned us that people would be hard to love. That is exactly what Jesus was addressing in the passage of scripture above as He taught his followers about loving others.

So let's **Give Up** that jealousy and let the Lord replace it with love for one another!

Chapter 5

Give Up Frustration

Give Up Frustration

My husband always says "we live in a microwave world", meaning that we live in a time of so much instant gratification that we don't know how to be patient. How could we learn patience when everything is literally at our fingertips?

At my age, I can actually remember when my family got our first microwave. I was a child, probably about 9 or 10 years old. My dad brought home this big contraption and he and my mom began showing my sister and me how it worked. I remember thinking it was some kind of magic! I mean this machine was able to cook things in a fraction of the time and effort that it would normally take. No more WAITING right?

Although I do believe the microwave was one of the best inventions in my lifetime, I can't help but think that it did begin an era when people expected things to be done faster.

Just like most any inventions of the last few decades, it was made to help people keep up with their fast pace lifestyle. Since then, we have had a ton of inventions that give us what we need with the push of a button. Computers, internet, smartphones... the list could go on and on.

Don't get me wrong, I am not condemning these things. I use them all myself, daily. The technology of the modern world can be very helpful and convenient. But I do believe that all of the "push of a button" conveniences that we have today have caused us to be **frustrated Christians.**

In our everyday lives, we rarely have to wait very long for things. And if we do we get so impatient and frustrated! Especially when it comes to food, right? I'm sure you can relate, just like me!

It is sad to say that we honestly don't know how to wait for things anymore. I can remember when I used to take pictures with my 35mm film camera.

I would drop the film off at the store to get the photos developed and anticipate what they were going to look like! When I would go pick them up and look through them, there were always some "duds". You know those photos that were blurry or just didn't take for whatever reason. But that didn't bother me because the photos I had been waiting on were so great! They were worth the wait! Now we don't even have to wait for great photos. We just delete the bad ones as soon as we take them. And we can use photoshop and filters to make the good ones even better. The point I'm trying to make is not that there is anything wrong with these new conveniences; it's that they have caused us to be impatient in life. That impatience has carried over into our spiritual lives! We know what the Bible says about waiting on the Lord, but it is so hard for us to do!

Wait on the Lord: be of good courage, and he shall strengthen thine heart: wait, I say, on the Lord.

(Psalm 27:14)

I read a book a few years ago by Kim Haney entitled God has a Waiting Room. The first time I read it was right before the storms with my boys had begun. Still, I could relate to this book very well based off of other circumstances in my life when I had to wait on the Lord's answers to my prayers. Since then, I have read this book two more times! It is so powerful! In the book she so perfectly explains the struggle that someone goes through in the "waiting room" of life. You know that time when you pray for something so desperately and have faith that the Lord is going to answer BUT you are still WAITING! There are no push button answers in God's waiting room! Aside from the Bible, this book had become my life manual for a while.

She explained and helped me to understand that it's not always about the answer to a specific prayer, but what we learn about ourselves while in the *waiting room* that is most important!

"My friend, if you find yourself in God's waiting room, don't resist it, don't cross your name off the waiting list, or skip out. Don't believe the lie that God is not hearing your prayers or will not answer; just realize you're in the waiting room. <u>In this season God is able to impart and reveal spiritual nuggets, things that come only to those who are willing to wait with Him.</u>"

\- Kim Haney

What I also learned from this book is that it's how we respond in the waiting room that makes the difference. Are we going to get so tired and frustrated that we give up on the promises that the Lord has given us, or will we hold on, believe, and trust the God that cannot lie?

But they that wait upon the Lord shall renew their strength; they shall mount up with wings as eagles; they shall run, and not be weary; they shall walk, and not faint.
(Isaiah 40:31)

When these storms that I am in with my kids started, I was praying for them and these situations, one day, and the Lord gave me a scripture of promise for my boys. I had been crying out to God that day on their behalf. I remember asking God in that prayer to just please give me something to hold on to. "Lord, just let me know that you heard me today." I don't know about you, but sometimes I just need that little glimmer of hope to keep my head up. When I opened my Bible that day, I opened directly to Isaiah chapter 54.

The Lord had actually given me this chapter years earlier during a very different battle that I was in. At that time it was like the words were speaking directly to me in my situation. So this day, when the Lord took me back to that chapter, I was a little confused. "Lord, how does this apply to my children?"

Then I read verse 13 and that was it! God is so faithful!

And all thy children shall be taught of the Lord; and great shall be the peace of thy children.
(Isaiah 54:13)

God is so good! I just kept reading and repeating and declaring; "Great shall be the PEACE of thy children!"

Like I have said before, this storm is not over, but I can say that I have seen the Lord working on their behalf so powerfully!

The tests and trials that they both are going through are very different for each of them, but I have no doubt that on the other side of this season, the Lord has that PERFECT PEACE waiting for them.

The reason I can be so sure of this is because the Bible says that if we pray for anything according to the will of God, that He hears us! ... AND if he hears us, we know we have the petitions that we desired of Him! Oh, what a glorious promise!

And this is the confidence that we have in him, that if we ask any thing according to his will, he heareth us: And we know that if he hear us, whatsoever we ask, we know that we have the petitions that we desired of him.
(1 John 5:14-15)

I was so excited about the second part of the verse the Lord gave me that day. (Isaiah 54:13)... *" great shall be the peace of thy children."* I am still excited about that part of my promise!

It keeps me going while I'm in this waiting room. But later when I was reading the verse again, I began to understand the beginning of that verse differently than I had before and it has made all the difference! *"All thy children shall be taught of the Lord;"*
When I started studying and looking at what this mean, I realized that it wasn't saying they would be taught "about" the Lord, but it meant they would be taught by the Lord!

The English Standard Version, **Isaiah 54:13 "All your children shall be taught by the Lord..."**

Oh my! This was so powerful to me! I know that right now while I'm in the waiting room, my children are living out this promise the Lord gave me!

They are being taught by the Lord! I can rest in this promise because I know the Lord loves them so much that he is teaching them some things and giving them their own powerful testimonies!

Let me encourage you today to **Give Up** the frustration that you are feeling! Maybe you are in God's Waiting Room right now. Just remember that there are no push button answers to our prayers. Rest in His promises that He will answer you in His perfect time!

I pray that if you have been frustrated that you haven't seen the answers to your prayers come to pass yet, that you would search the scriptures for yourself for that promise of hope to hold on to. The Bible is full of beautiful promises from the Lord to his children! Pray and ask the Lord to give you something personal to your situation. Our God is so faithful that I have no doubt that He will do it for you just as He did me!

I have a notebook that I began writing scriptures in that I felt like were promises of hope for me during this time of waiting. I am sharing a few of them with you in hopes that they will be a help to someone reading this. Even though I have made them personal for me, they are not just mine!

God's word is so powerful and His promises are true for us all!

Psalm 73:28 "But it is good for me to draw near to God: I have put my trust in the Lord God, that I may declare all thy works."

Psalm 4:3 "Offer the sacrifices of righteousness, and put your trust in the Lord."

Isaiah 26.3 "Thou wilt keep him in perfect peace whose mind is stayed on thee: because he trusteth in thee."

Psalm 34:1 "I will bless the Lord at all times: his praise shall continually be in my mouth."

Philippians 4:7 "And the peace of God which passeth all understanding, shall keep your hearts and minds through Christ Jesus."

Romans 15:13 " Now the God of hope fill you with all joy and peace in believing that ye may abound in hope, through the power of the Holy Ghost."

Chapter 6

Give Up

the Past

Give Up the Past

Our memory is a very strange part of us isn't it? Many times it seems as though the things that we would like to remember, like where we put our car keys, are somewhere lost in our mind, and no matter how hard we try to recall them, we just can't. Then there are those moments in life that we wish so desperately that we could forget! I will not try to convince you that I am any kind of expert on the way our mind or memory works, because that is definitely not true. I have no doubt that we all have things about our past that we would love to forget. I know I do! Although on our own, it is impossible to break away from our past, I am so thankful that with God's help we can *forget those things which are behind!*

Brethren, I count not myself to have apprehended: but this one thing I do, forgetting those things which are behind, and reaching forth unto those things which are before, I press toward the mark for the prize of the high calling of God in Christ Jesus.
(Philippians 3:13-14)

I do believe that when Paul was writing these verses to the Christians in Philippi, that he was speaking to people who had things in their past that they needed to forget or **Give Up**. Just like you and me, those people who had begun a new life in the Lord, had things holding them back from their past. Yes, there are times that I believe with a lot of prayer and renewing of our mind, the Lord will help us forget some of those painful memories. I also believe from my own experience that there are some memories that were so traumatic, so painful that it may be impossible to actually forget. *Those are the times when we must make a specific effort to **Give Up** our past!*

Some of the most powerfully used people in the Bible had a past that they had to **Give Up** to the Lord!

Paul, who was formerly named Saul, was ruthless in his quest to rid the world of Christians. He tortured them, threw them in prison, and even murdered them!

When he had his encounter with the Lord that day on the road to Damascus, his life changed forever! Everything about Saul changed that day, even his name! Paul spent the rest of his life completely dedicated to the Lord, spreading the gospel of Christ. He is known as one of the greatest examples of God's mercy, and love!

Simon Peter publicly denied even knowing Jesus, not just once but three times! And to make matters worse, this was after Jesus Christ himself had warned him that it was going to happen! The great news is that Peter went on to repent of his sins and accepted forgiveness from the Lord. He then spent the rest of his life preaching the gospel to reach thousands of people!

The Bible even tells us that Jesus gave Peter the plan of salvation, which he stood up and preached on the day of Pentecost.

Then Peter said unto them, Repent, and be baptized every one of you in the name of Jesus Christ for the remission of sins, and ye shall receive the gift of the Holy Ghost.   *(Acts 2:38)*

David is known as one of the most influential figures of the Bible. We know him as the man after God's own heart. Every time I read the beautiful Psalms that he wrote to the Lord, I am inspired by his love for God! It's hard to imagine that he failed the Lord, so miserably, in his lifetime. I mean, I know that he lied, cheated, planned, and carried through with a murder. But when I think of David, those are not the things I remember about him! Why? Why was David able to come back from such a horrible past and be used so mightily by the Lord? It's because he was able to humble himself and truly repent of his sins.

He is a great example of how someone was able to **Give Up** their past to the Lord and accept the beautiful future that God placed in front him!

I could go on and on telling about numerous other people from the Bible that had a very troubled past but went on to do mighty things for the Lord.

The point I'm trying to make to you is... we all have a past that we're not proud of. Maybe you have been so scarred by your past that you simply can't forget. If so, I have some wonderful news for you! You may not be able to forget, but you can **Give Up** those painful memories to the Lord! And when you do, the Bible tells us that the Lord WILL FORGET THEM!

He will turn again, he will have compassion upon us; he will subdue our iniquities; and thou wilt cast all their sins into the depths of the sea.
(Micah 7:19)

<u>The devil loves to remind us of our past, but when he does, just remember that the Lord has cast it into the depths of sea to remember it no more!</u>

Scars

When I was seven years old my dad and I had a car accident. We were traveling on our narrow gravel road that we lived on at the time and came to a steep curve. At the same time, there was a truck coming around the curve in the opposite direction. Neither my dad nor the other driver had time to stop and we collided head on. It was before the days that we knew the importance of seatbelts, so I was thrown head first into the windshield. I remember seeing a red blur (which I learned was the color of the other vehicle). The next thing I remember was waking up in my mother's arms on the way to the hospital. Once we got to the local ER, they ended up sending me directly to Lebonheur Children's Hospital. There I received around 15 stitches in my forehead. The protecting hand of God was on me that day!

We were so blessed that my injuries were minor compared to what they could have been. But it has been 40 years since this happened and I still carry the scars. They are much less noticeable, now, than they used to be, maybe even unnoticed my most people that I meet. But when I see them, instead of remembering all of the fear and confusion that I'm sure I felt that day as a seven year old little girl, *I am reminded of God's grace! I'm reminded of my future instead of my past!*

*I believe we all carry scars

from our pasts.

Some are more noticeable than others.

I pray that the next time you notice

those scars that you carry,

you would be reminded of the loving grace

of God instead of

the pain that caused them!

I want to encourage you today; don't let the regrets of your past hold you back from a bright and promising future that the Lord has prepared for you!

Don't hold your head down in shame or regret, but allow the Lord to lift up your head toward Him!

But thou, O Lord, art a shield for me; my glory, and the lifter up of mine head.   (Psalm 3:3)

For I know the plans I have for you, declares the Lord, plans to prosper you and not to harm you, plans to give you hope and a future.
(Jeremiah 29:11 NIV)

Chapter 7

Give Up Negativity

Give Up Negativity

I want to talk to you about something that I believe is one of the most damaging mind sets that is so easy to get sucked into. The fact that it is so contagious makes it dangerous for us as Christians who are supposed to be following Christ's example. I am talking about having a negative or complaining attitude.

I do consider myself to be a pretty positive person overall. Do I have days when everything seems to go wrong? Absolutely, but I'm also at a point in my life that I realize how truly blessed I am. However, that does not keep me from falling into that negative mindset on occasion. I mean it is so easy to do isn't it? I can be having a normal conversation with someone, and before I realize it one of us mentions something negative about a situation and it's like a snowball effect! Once the complaining starts, it doesn't stop until we have built this huge pile of excuses as to why things are simply not as they should be!

Almost always when this happens to me, I think back to that conversation and am so convicted about my ability to be so ungrateful for the blessings in my life. I'm sure you can relate. I mean, after all, we are still flesh and as much as we would love to think that we are spiritually above such nonsense, we simply aren't. The good news is, though, that we serve a merciful God who WILL convict us and receive our prayer of repentance when this happens. The Bible says His mercy and compassion toward us is made new every morning! Wow! What a mighty God we serve that He recognizes that we are flesh and we do need His grace and mercy daily!

It is of the Lord's mercies that we are not consumed, because his compassions fail not. They are new every morning: great is thy faithfulness. *(Lamentations 3:22-23)*

Having said this, we don't ever need to take the Lord's mercy for granted. Don't make the mistake of thinking that this type of negative attitude and behavior is not sinful. It most definitely is! I believe it truly breaks the Lord's heart when He hears His children complaining.

Especially when He knows how good He has been to us!

I know when I hear my own children complain about simple things, it is so disappointing as a parent. We all want to raise children who grow up to be thankful for the things they have. It has always been so eye opening for my kids and me whenever we have been able to take trips to Mexico to visit family over the years. Some of the places and circumstances that we have witnessed while there are so humbling to say the least. Many live in far worse conditions than we do, yet I have never heard them complain.

On the contrary, most of them are so thankful for the basics in life, like food and shelter. I have always tried to use those experiences to remind my children of how blessed we are.

So we know that if it bothers us as parents to hear our children have a negative attitude or complain, then it must break the Lord's heart when we do the same!

The children of Israel had this same complaining spirit and it kept them from receiving their promise from the Lord for forty years! Lord help us!

And when the people complained, it displeased the Lord: and the Lord heard it; and his anger was kindled...   (Numbers 11:1)

We all have promises from the Lord that we are praying and believing the Lord for. We so desperately want to see them come to pass. How sad it would be if our negative or complaining attitude is keeping us from seeing those promises!

The truth is that we serve a God that is so great and powerful! If we truly examine our lives, it is easy to see the blessings of the Lord upon us! So let's not let ourselves get caught up in that negative conversation. Let's make a conscious effort to turn them into something positive and something to be thankful for! This is what the Lord desires and deserves from us as his children. He deserves all of the praise and thanksgiving that we can give!

*After all, our worst day as a Christian is so much better than our best day was as a lost sinner. Why? Because we have the hope of a beautiful eternity that awaits us with our Lord and Savior Jesus Christ!

*Here are just a few scriptures that remind us of the importance of thanking and praising God.

I will bless the Lord at all times: his praise shall continually be in my mouth.
O magnify the Lord with me, let us exalt his name together.
(Psalm 34:1&3)

How excellent is thy loving kindness, O God! therefore the children of men put their trust under the shadow of thy wings.
(Psalm 36:7)

In every thing give thanks: for this is the will of God in Christ Jesus concerning you.
(1 Thessalonians 5:18)

Let every thing that hath breath praise the Lord. Praise ye the Lord.
(Psalm 150:6)

Chapter 8

Give Up Bitterness

Give Up Bitterness

I once heard someone say that holding onto bitterness toward someone is like drinking poison and expecting them to die. What a true and powerful statement. We have such a misconception that somehow holding on to that bitterness that we feel toward them is punishing them. When in reality, the majority of the time, those people who have hurt us are not touched by our inability to forgive them. On the contrary, holding on to all of the bitterness and pain that we feel is poisoning our own spirit. In the long run, we are the only person who is hurt by our unwillingness to forgive!

I am so thankful that the Lord was able to teach me this powerful truth about myself through my own circumstances.

I have received my fair share of pain and heartache over the years, as I'm sure many of you have. One thing I learned fairly quickly though, is that I don't like the "bitter me". If you have ever battled with being bitter toward someone, then you can relate. It will turn you into someone that you don't recognize. At least that has been my experience.

I felt angry, yet the anger didn't bring me any kind of relief. I would try to convince myself that my feelings were justified, but that would only make me feel helpless in my situation because I knew the person who hurt me didn't care. I also realized that as long as I was holding on to the hate and pain that they caused, I would always be bound to them. Even though I had cut off all ties with them physically, I was still tied to them by those emotional chains of bitterness.

Isn't it amazing how prayer changes things?

When I decided to pray about it, instead of feeling sorry for myself, the Lord was able to comfort me and help me to realize that I didn't have to hold on to all of the pain!

I was able to see that it was possible to **Give Up** my bitterness to the Lord! When I did, I received that comfort that only the Lord can give! The chains that still had me bound to them were finally broken.

I want you to understand that when we decide to forgive someone it is not for their benefit, but for ours! There is a freedom that comes along with truly letting go of the pain that someone else caused! The Bible tells us that God is our **Comforter**!

Blessed be God, even the Father of our Lord Jesus Christ, the Father of mercies, and <u>the God of all comfort;</u>
Who comforts us in all our tribulation, that we may be able to comfort them which are in any trouble...
(2 Corinthians 1:3-4)

I want to share a story with you from someone who has faced a great deal of pain and mistreatment in her lifetime. Out of respect for her privacy she chooses to remain anonymous. I pray that her testimony will help someone to **Give Up** the bitterness in their life, just as she has done.

```
My first recollection of pain and
betrayal from someone who was supposed
to love and care about me came early in
my life.
```

At the age of five I was molested by a close family member. The roller coaster of emotions that a young child feels when someone they love takes advantage of them is hard to describe. First came the confusion. At that young age, I really didn't even know what was happening at first. I just knew it was wrong. The emotions that I had always felt toward this person BEFORE were of love and adoration. After the confusion and the understanding of just how wrong the things that were being done to me were, came the pain of betrayal. Lastly, came the hate and bitterness toward this person.

When I entered my teenage years, just at that confusing time in a girl's life when my hormones and emotions were all over the map, came my second betrayal. This time it was another close family member who took advantage of me sexually.

Again, all those emotions of confusion, pain, and so much bitterness came flooding in. By this time I was beginning to question myself. What was I doing to cause these people to hurt me this way? I mean there's no way this should have happened again unless the problem was ME! By this point, I had completely shut down emotionally when it came to any men in my life besides my dad. I knew how much both my parents loved me. They did find out about the first instance at the age of five, and I saw how devastated they were by it and how much guilt and pain it caused them that they never knew it was happening. I don't really know why I never told them about the second person as a young teen, except that I knew it would cause so many problems in our extended family and I didn't ever want to see them hurt like that again.

I know it doesn't sound logical now but as a confused teenager, it made the most sense at the time. I did distance myself from this person on my own and eventually cut them out of my life. Again came all the hate and bitterness. I don't really know how I was able to hide my pain so well for the next several years but I did. I came from a good home with loving parents who did everything they could to give me a good upbringing. Looking back, maybe I masked it so well because no one would have expected me to have this kind of past based on my raising. So I hid it well. But deep inside I hated those men who had betrayed my trust so horribly. I went on to do well in high school in sports and academics. On the outside, I seemed to have it all together, but on the inside I was fighting a horrible battle with all of the bitterness that I could not let go of.

It was something I just settled in my mind that I was always going to deal with. It was eating me up inside. It was a part of the real me that nobody knew. I look back now and see how miserable I was with my life and myself. It wasn't until I gave my life to the Lord a few years after college that I was finally able to let go of the pain of my past! It was then that I let Jesus take all of the hate and bitterness toward those men and replace it with His love and acceptance! I don't know how to adequately describe the freedom that I felt that day. I just knew that I had carried this thing with me for so many years that had eaten away at my soul, and for the first time since I was five years old I felt innocent again! Innocent because I had let God's love wash me completely clean.

Not only did He cleanse me from my sins, but from the guilt and shame that came from my past!

I wish I could tell you that my pain and betrayal ended there, but that was not the case. A few years later I ended up in a marriage where I suffered through the pain of infidelity as well as verbal and emotional abuse. I am thankful that I was able to escape from that relationship. Although that was a horrible time in my life, I can honestly say that I never let bitterness for him settle in my heart. I was finally at a point in my walk with God that I knew the importance of forgiveness. Never again did I want to let the actions of another person determine my happiness. So I chose to forgive. Not for him, but for me!

*I hope and pray that you can take away from this testimony the importance of forgiveness and **Giving Up** the bitterness in our lives!

I realize that there may be someone reading this that has been through similar circumstances. Maybe you have suffered through things that no one else knows about. You have built up a wall that keeps you from truly breaking free from that person because you think if you forgive them you are somehow not holding them responsible for your pain any longer. I pray today that I could help you realize that forgiving them, has nothing to do with them and their guilt. But it is your willingness to let God take that pain and bitterness out of your heart so that He can replace it with pure emotions, like peace, love, and joy.

When we completely give our heart, mind, and soul to the Lord, it allows us to break free from those damaging emotions, and finally break free from the person who hurt us!

Now the God of hope fill you with all joy and peace in believing, that ye may abound in hope, through the power of the Holy Ghost.
(Romans 15:13)

* **The Lord commands us to forgive.**

Yes, there is a freedom that comes along with letting go of bitterness when we choose to forgive someone who has wronged us. I believe the reason we feel that freedom and peace is because we are <u>obeying the Lord</u>. The Bible is full of scriptures about forgiveness. Not only forgiveness that the Lord shows toward us, but scriptures about forgiving others.

And be ye kind one to another, tender hearted, forgiving one another, even as God for Christ's sake hath forgiven you.
(Ephesians 4:32)

For If ye forgive men their trespasses, your Heavenly Father will also forgive you.
(Matthew 6:14)

Then Peter came to him, and said, Lord, how oft shall my brother sin against me, and I forgive him? Till seven times?
Jesus saith unto him, I say not unto thee, Until seven times: but, Until seventy times seven.
(Matthew 18:21-22 NIV)

Please don't misunderstand the point I'm trying to make. Jesus tells us that we must forgive others. He does not tell us that we must continue any kind of relationship with them. Remember that forgiveness is about you and your walk with the Lord. It is not about your relationship with the person who hurt you. I understand that there are circumstances when we must completely cut ties with people.

I also understand that sometimes forgiveness is a process. I don't believe that true forgiveness always happens instantly.

When I told you about how I was able to pray about the bitterness that I felt toward the people who hurt me, and give it to the Lord, I was not implying that it happened during one prayer.

It did take some time, but I knew that I did want to obey the Lord and break free of the pain!

I pray that you would be able to as well!

Chapter 9

Give Up Excuses

Give Up Excuses

I have always been intrigued by the Bible story of Mary and Martha. I think it is because I can relate to both of them and the situation that they found themselves in. This story is told in only four verses so let me refresh your memory so we can dive deeper into this passage.

As Jesus and his disciples were on their way, he came to a village where a woman named Martha opened her home to him. She had a sister called Mary, who sat at the Lord's feet listening to what he said. But Martha was distracted by all the preparations that had to be made. She came to him and asked, Lord, don't you care that my sister has left me to do the work by myself? Tell her to help me.
Martha, Martha, the Lord answered, you are worried and upset about many things, but few things are needed - or indeed only one.
Mary has chosen what is better, and it will not be taken away from her. (Luke 10:38-42 NIV)

I have always known that Mary is who I want to pattern my Christian walk after.

Who doesn't want to sit at the feet of Jesus, listening and learning from the Master? We all do, right? Although I realize Mary chose the best part that day, I can relate to Martha so well. Chances are, so can you! We live such a fast paced life. We have become masters at multitasking. I feel like that was how Martha felt that day. After all Jesus Christ was visiting her home! Can you imagine everything that must have been going through her mind that day? Of course she wanted to serve Him her very best dish. I have no doubt that she had been working so hard to make sure her house was clean and looked the best it ever had. I'm sure I'm not the only one who can relate. We know how it feels don't we, to wake up one morning to a house that looks like Hurricane Katrina passed through the night before, only to find out that company will be there for dinner!

Not just any company, but someone that you love and respect so much that you want to put your best foot forward. This was Martha that day!

She was working so hard only to look over and find her sister sitting at Jesus's feet, so cozy, listening to all He had to say. I can't help but think that Martha would have loved to be sitting right there beside Mary that day, but she chose not to. It really all comes down to priorities, doesn't it? That day Mary's top priority was Jesus! I know the Bible doesn't tell us this, but I doubt that Mary was just being lazy and trying to skip out on helping her sister. I just think that she wanted to be in His presence so much that she simply **chose the best part!**

So when Martha confronted Jesus with the situation and wanted Him to intervene and tell Mary to get up and help, Jesus reminded her that Mary had made the better choice that day. Mary could have made the excuse that she needed to go help her sister with all the work that needed to be done, but she didn't. **She chose Jesus!**

Not just serving Jesus like Martha, but listening and learning from Him. I really love the ending of this passage when Jesus is telling Martha that Mary has made the best choice. He said, *"and it will not be taken from her."* You see, Jesus knew that any time that Mary spent at His feet was not wasted time. It was important time that would never be taken from her. So any time that we can sit at His feet and listen, we will learn things that can never be taken from us!

In this Christian walk, with all of our many church functions and activities that go on, sometimes it is so easy to make the excuse of serving. I really love serving others. I love being about my Father's business. This passage in the Bible that is only four verses long, hits me straight in the heart though. I know the Lord put this story in there for us "Marthas" who desire to be Mary!

I am thankful that God has a way of teaching us to **Give Up** all the excuses that we make for not spending time with Him! As I have told you, I have been in a stormy season lately. During these past two years, I have learned to **Give Up** my excuses for not spending the time with God that I need. Although before this storm, I did take time daily to pray and read my Bible, God still knows how to get our attention when He wants more of us and our time. I can honestly say that while fighting this battle, I have grown so much closer to the Lord. I want to propose some questions to you that I had to answer for myself.

* What if all the pain and confusion that you are going through right now is the best thing that could have happened to you spiritually?

*What if you are going to come out of this stronger than ever?

*What if God is using this to build your faith in Him?

*What if this is all part of His great plan for your life?

If the answer to all of these questions is YES, would you still make that excuse not to wake up early to spend that much needed time with Him?

My answer to that last question is "No".
I choose to say no to the excuses.

Job

When I think of a person who could have made so many excuses to give up on God, I think of Job. He was literally living his best life when, out of nowhere, the Lord allowed Satan to touch him. You can read the whole story in the book of Job. I would recommend this story to anyone who is struggling with making excuses for living for God.

The Bible tells us that God gave Satan permission to afflict Job because HE knew that Job could handle anything that came his way. God only told Satan that he could not take Job's life. Wow! What a relationship with the Lord that Job must have had for God to have that much confidence in him?

From that point forward Job suffered unthinkable trials and tribulations. He lost everything he had. He lost his children, his material possessions, and his health. Yet, Job never complained one time! Even his wife told him how foolish he was to still serve God. Job had so many opportunities to make excuses for why he could not serve the Lord anymore. However, instead of making excuses, we find him lifting up praise and thanksgiving to the Lord!

...The Lord gave and the Lord hath taken away; blessed be the name of the Lord.
(Job 1:21)

So the next time we find ourselves making excuses for why we can't spend time with, or serve, the Lord sufficiently, let's remember Mary and Job.

*They both made the best choice in their situation.

They chose to **GiveUp** the excuses and embrace their relationship with God!

I pray that we would do the same!

Chapter 10

Conclusion

Conclusion

What a journey this has been! This book has been in my heart for many years. I can remember having a conversation with my husband during the first few years of our marriage that I felt like I needed to write a book. It's funny how God works because I didn't even have a clear idea what it would be about. I only had that nudge from the Lord that I needed to do it. Isai has always been supportive of any of my goals in life. When we talked about it, he told me that he believed I could do it. It has been close to 15 years since that conversation and I have tried to begin writing several times over the years, only to hit a road block in my mind and spirit.

I understand now that it was not the right time during all those other attempts. Many of the testimonies that I have shared with you, have happened <u>after</u> I felt that first pull toward writing it. When I began writing recently about the "vision" the Lord was showing me about the girl in the ocean (me), it really wasn't meant to become a book. I thought it was only going to be something that I would share with the ladies at my home church.

I was praying that I could help encourage some of them who might be going through some struggles of their own. But God had other plans. This time that I began to type out the things that were in my heart, that road block never came! It was quite the opposite. There were thoughts and feelings coming into my mind so fast, at times, that I was just praying I would not forget the next thought before I had a chance to make a note of it. Then I realized that this was it! This was the book that the Lord put in my spirit all those years ago! **God's timing is perfect!** When I told my husband that I felt like I had finally started *the book*, that's exactly what he told me. "All those other times were not the right time."

This has been, by far, one of the scariest and most challenging things I have ever done! If I'm honest with you and myself, I can say that there were a few moments that I was doubting if I should really be this open about some of the emotional struggles I've had. I have felt very vulnerable.

That's a feeling that none of us are comfortable with. But like I have said before, my desire for this book is that I could help someone who may be struggling too. I believe we all go through tests and trials in life for a reason. God has a purpose for every season that we go through!

I pray that the Lord would use my struggles to help you find a purpose in yours!

I would like to share some notes from each chapter that I hope will stick with you.

Chapter 1- The Struggle

There is a difference between <u>faith</u> and <u>trust</u>. In my mind and my walk with God, I had always used these words as if they meant basically the same things. I have even substituted one word for the other.

But what I have learned is that <u>faith</u> is believing that God **can** and even **will** answer my prayer, but <u>trust</u> is actually handing my problem over to Him and trusting Him completely to do it. WITHOUT MY HELP! OUCH!

Chapter 2- Give Up Confusion

If you are dealing with confusion of any kind in your life right now, I want to encourage you to resist it by praying and seeking the Lord with all of your heart. And allow the Lord to take that brokenness you have experienced and use it to make you into someone new!

Chapter 3- *Give Up Worthlessness*

Let me encourage you today that you have so much Worth! This book is about "Giving Up", to the Lord, those things that are holding us back from living the life that God has planned for us.

So let's Give Up that pain, fear, doubt, and yes, WORTHLESSNESS! And in return the Lord will give us His love, peace, and purpose in life!

Chapter 4- *Give Up Jealousy*

Life is not a competition!

Yes, it is a race, but we

are all on the same team!

We are all working

toward the same goal!

So let's help and encourage one another along the way!

Chapter 5- Give Up Frustration

Give Up the frustration that you are feeling! Maybe you are in God's Waiting Room right now; but just remember that there are no push button answers to our prayers. Rest in His promises that He will answer you in His perfect time!

Chapter 6- Give Up the Past

We all have a past that we're not proud of. Maybe you have been so scarred by your past that you simply can't forget. If so I have some wonderful news for you! You may not be able to forget, but you can **Give Up** those painful memories to the Lord! And when you do, the Bible tells us that the Lord WILL FORGET THEM!

He will turn again, he will have compassion upon us; he will subdue our iniquities; and thou wilt cast all their sins into the depths of the sea.

(Micah 7:19)

Chapter 7- Give Up Negativity

After all, our worst day as a Christian is so much better than our best day was as a lost sinner. Why? Because we have the Hope of a beautiful eternity that awaits us with our Lord and Savior Jesus Christ!

Chapter 8- Give Up Bitterness

Holding on to all of the bitterness and pain that we feel is poisoning our own spirit. In the long run, we are the only person who is hurt by our unwillingness to forgive!

Chapter 9- Give Up Excuses

So the next time we find ourselves making excuses for why we can't spend time with, or serve, the Lord sufficiently, let's remember Mary and Job. They both made the best choice in their situation. They chose to Give Up the excuses and embrace their relationship with God! I pray that we would do the same!

I would like to end this book with a prayer for you.

Dear God,

I want to thank you for every person who took their time to read this book. Lord, I know that life can be so difficult at times, but I pray that you would bring strength and courage to the lives of these precious people. Help them to be able to Give Up to You, all of the difficult emotions that they are struggling with. I pray that they would recognize your loving voice and allow you to give them the security of your hand that is always patiently waiting. In Jesus Name I pray, AMEN.